English 4

Practice in the Basic Skills

Contents

Nouns

A Write out the **nouns** in each of these sentences.

1 The dog ran away over the field.

2 The bananas and custard were in a dish.

3 Elephants are used to carry logs.

4 Wine is made from grapes.

5 The police officer stopped all cars and lorries.

6 The children and teachers enjoyed the circus.

7 The lifeguard swam to the struggling swimmer.

8 Last night Tom read a book and went for a walk.

9 Porridge, sausages, egg and toast make a big breakfast.

10 The helicopter landed safely on a football field behind a school.

B Here are the meanings of ten **nouns**. They all begin with the letter **c**.

e.g. a long, green vegetable used in salads　　　**cucumber**

1 A bird that lays its eggs in other birds' nests.

2 The roof of a room.

3 Cement, sand, stones and water mixed together.

4 A drink made from apple juice.

5 A person who buys from a shop.

6 A child of your uncle or aunt.

7 A machine for lifting heavy objects.

8 A food made from sour milk.

9 A list of the days, weeks and months of the year.

10 The grub from which a moth or butterfly comes.

Adjectives (1)

A   Write out the **adjectives** in these sentences.

   1   The weather was damp and foggy.

   2   The blind dog was found near the wooden bridge.

   3   Peter is short and fat, but Sam is tall and slim.

   4   Tigers are large, powerful, striped cats found in Asia.

   5   The small yacht battled against strong winds and a rough sea.

   6   Magpies have slender, long tails and short wings.

   7   The fast, thrilling race excited the large crowd.

   8   The fisherman wore a thick, blue sweater and a red, woollen hat.

   9   Dodos are extinct, flightless birds which looked like giant pigeons.

 10   The brave explorers were exhausted after their dangerous journey through the hot, humid jungle.

B   Choose the correct **adjective** from the list to complete each sentence.

empty	victorious	fatal	nourishing	huge
courageous	priceless	fragrant	difficult	fierce

   1   A .... painting was stolen from the art gallery.

   2   A .... accident occurred on the mountain.

   3   The .... dog bit the boy.

   4   .... roses are very pleasant in a garden.

   5   Their voices echoed in the .... room.

   6   The .... whale opened its mouth and swallowed the boat.

   7   The .... firefighter rescued the old man from the blazing house.

   8   The .... team was given a great welcome by the town.

   9   The general had to make a .... decision.

 10   After five days adrift on a raft the sailor enjoyed a .... meal.

C   Now use each of these **adjectives** in sentences of your own.

Verbs (1)

A Write out the **verbs** in these sentences.

1 The old lady slipped then fell on the icy road.

2 When Holly finished her book she returned it to the library.

3 Paul ate his breakfast quickly then ran to school.

4 It took Mark two hours to make his model aeroplane.

5 After the keeper fed the lions she cleaned the monkey's cage.

6 In the morning mum baked cakes, cleaned the windows and washed some clothes.

7 I saw the helicopter rescue two bathers from the sea.

8 The racing car sped along the straight, but braked too hard on the bend and skidded into bales of straw.

9 The astronauts climbed into their capsule and checked their controls.

10 Poor Sophie fell off her bike and broke her arm.

B Choose the correct **verb** from the list to complete each sentence.

perched	repeated	flickered	collided	marooned
measured	collapsed	interrupted	swooped	shattered

1 Mandy carefully _____ the length of the corridor.

2 The two ships _____ in the fog.

3 The kestrel _____ on its prey.

4 I saw the parrot _____ on the top branch of the tree.

5 When Anni finished the race she _____ on the track.

6 The candle _____ in the draughty cellar.

7 The ball hit the window and _____ the glass.

8 The teacher _____ the question but still Simon didn't know the answer.

9 The rude boy _____ his dad when he was on the telephone.

10 Robinson Crusoe was _____ on a desert island.

C Now use each of these **verbs** in sentences of your own.

Adverbs (1)

A   Write out the **adverbs** in these sentences.

1   The cat climbed swiftly up the tree.

2   The dog barked loudly at the boys.

3   The sun shone brightly for the carnival.

4   Grandad was sitting comfortably in his chair.

5   Our school sports day takes place annually.

6   The tired old lady walked wearily up the hill.

7   The farmer walked slowly across the field but when he saw the injured cow he ran quickly towards it.

8   The teacher remembered clearly that Alex's homework was not given in on time.

9   The leopard sprang suddenly from the tree but the antelope cleverly avoided it.

10   John came immediately but Mark arrived late.

B   Choose the correct **adverb** from the list to complete each sentence.

soundly	anxiously	fiercely	correctly	tunefully
foolishly	bitterly	silently	frantically	briefly

1   Helen answered the question ....

2   When Tom was on holiday he spent his money ....

3   After their long walk on the hills the children slept ....

4   Peter was trapped in the mud and he shouted ....

5   The guard dog growled .... when he heard a noise.

6   Carolyn had to explain .... because she was in a hurry.

7   The burglar crept .... up the stairs.

8   Crowds of people waited .... for news of the overdue aircraft.

9   Our choir sang .... in the concert.

10   Jane cried .... when her bicycle was stolen.

C   Now use each **adverb** in sentences of your own.

Alphabetical order

A Write the names of these objects in alphabetical order.

B Write the following lines of words in alphabetical order.

   1   cage   runway   warrior   hobby   meat   beach

   2   nylon   smell   acorn   grass   white   quiz

   3   vein   puzzle   cry   jelly   duck   frost

C Write the names of these objects that begin with s in alphabetical order.

D Write the following lines of words in alphabetical order.

   1   potato   pea   public   pier   prize   path

   2   bite   boat   bread   bed   black   bulb

   3   witch   wrist   worm   whip   wasp   weak

E Write the names of these objects that begin with c in alphabetical order.

F Write the following lines of words in alphabetical order.

   1   spun   speak   spy   spin   spoon   spade

   2   prison   prime   prize   price   pride   princess

   3   channel   chalk   chatter   chameleon   chain   chart

Sentences

A Write the following so that the **beginnings** are matched with the correct **endings**.

beginning   ending

1   The man is putting his hat   so Jean put up her umbrella.

2   Dad is wearing a watch   at the signal.

3   Sam is painting   to rescue the sailors.

4   It was raining heavily   on his wrist.

5   The train is stopping   at Manchester Airport.

6   Nicky is cutting bread   on his head.

7   The aeroplane is landing   with a knife.

8   The lifeboat is speeding   the back door.

B Use your own words to **end** the following:

1   Paul tried very hard ....

2   There was great excitement at the zoo ....

3   Zara was very sad when ....

4   Just as Simon opened the door ....

5   Everyone dashed for cover when ....

C Use your own words at the **beginning** to make complete sentences.

1   .... so we ran off as fast as we could.

2   .... because the roads were so icy.

3   .... and we built a huge bonfire.

4   .... with all his strength.

5   .... but the keys were found.

Compound words

A   Write the name of each picture. Show the two words which form the **compound word**.

e.g. **neck** + **lace**   **necklace**

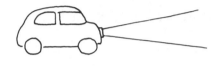
1

2

3

4

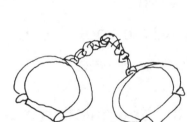
5

6

7

8

9

10

11

12

B   Write down another **compound word** beginning with the first part of the word you have written for each picture.

e.g. **1 head**land or **head**line

Vocabulary and spelling (1)

A The first letters of the answers spell out a **country**.

frozen water	— — —
a place where light meals are served	— — f —
the largest living land animal	— — e — — — — —
a place where books are kept	— — — r — — —
all the letters from A to Z	— — — — a — — —
a frightening dream	— — g — — — — — —
a yellow wild flower	— — n — — — — — —

B The first letters of the answers spell out a **mammal**.

a powerful machine for levelling ground	— u — — — — z — —
very old	— — — i — — —
to get out of the way	— o — — —
a slow-moving river of ice	— — — c — — —
a bird of prey	— — — l —
a large cattle farm	— — — — h

C The first letters of the answers spell out a **fruit**.

the eighth month of the year	— — — u — —
used to write with	— — n
wealthy	— — — h
a very young child	— — f — — —
a person who buys from a shop	— — — t — — — —
a sea animal with eight legs	— — — o — — —
the shape made by joining three straight sides	— — — a — — — —

Singular and plural

The names of the things illustrated below are nouns that form their **plurals** in different ways. Write down each noun, together with its **plural** form.

e.g. **wolf - wolves**

1

2

3

4

5

6

7

8

9

10

11

12

13

14

15

Mixed bag (1)

Your dictionary will help you to answer these.

A Write the **opposites** to these words.

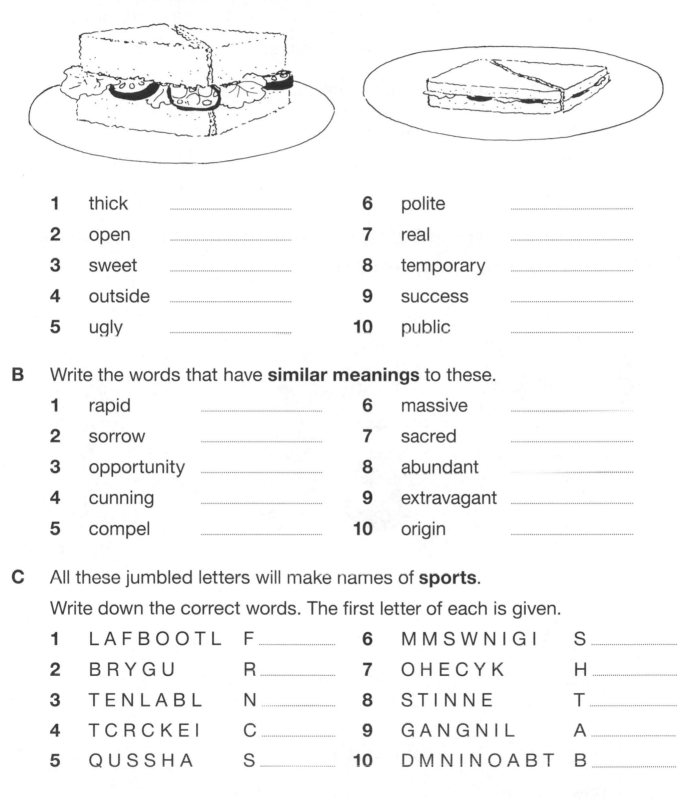

1	thick	....
2	open	....
3	sweet	....
4	outside	....
5	ugly	....

6	polite	....
7	real	....
8	temporary	....
9	success	....
10	public	....

B Write the words that have **similar meanings** to these.

1	rapid	....
2	sorrow	....
3	opportunity	....
4	cunning	....
5	compel	....

6	massive	....
7	sacred	....
8	abundant	....
9	extravagant	....
10	origin	....

C All these jumbled letters will make names of **sports**.

Write down the correct words. The first letter of each is given.

1	L A F B O O T L	F.........
2	B R Y G U	R.........
3	T E N L A B L	N.........
4	T C R C K E I	C.........
5	Q U S S H A	S.........

6	M M S W N I G I	S.........
7	O H E C Y K	H.........
8	S T I N N E	T.........
9	G A N G N I L	A.........
10	D M N I N O A B T	B.........

Gender

A   Write the **masculine** forms of these nouns.

1   grandmother   **4**   manageress   **7**   sow

2   stewardess   **5**   mare   **8**   duchess

3   peahen   **6**   headmistress   **9**   nun

B   Write the **feminine** forms of these nouns.

1   actor   **4**   stepdad   **7**   widower

2   stag   **5**   male   **8**   father-in-law

3   gentleman   **6**   colt   **9**   aunty

C   In each pair illustrated below there is one **masculine** and one **feminine**.
         Write out the correct names of each.

Picture story

Look carefully at the pictures then write a story that tells all that happened. Think of a title.

These words will help you.

river bridge watching snapped fall panic swimming
desperate drowning weir unconscious revive ambulance mayor
award bravery proud

Verbs (2)

Past tense

A Complete these sentences by using the **past tense** of the verb in brackets.

   1 Tom felt proud when he _____ hands with the team captain.   (shake)

   2 Miriam _____ on to the bank of the river until help came.   (hold)

   3 The cat _____ on to the bird table.   (spring)

   4 The town hall clock _____ seven and Jayne hadn't arrived.   (strike)

   5 Sonia _____ a letter of thanks to the librarian.   (write)

   6 The cars and buses _____ at the traffic lights.   (stop)

   7 I _____ swimming _____ the best of all sports.   (think, is)

   8 We _____ down to Tenby and _____ all the hotels _____ full.   (drive, find, are)

   9 I _____ to a football match and afterwards I _____ a meal.   (go, have)

   10 Mark's nose _____ a lot when he _____ off his bicycle.   (bleed, fall)

Past participle

B Use the **participle** of the verb in brackets to complete each sentence.

   1 The old man was _____ to be homeless. (know)

   2 Martin had _____ for a long walk. (go)

   3 Mo's ankle was _____ after the game. (swell)

   4 The jewels were _____ under the floorboards. (hide)

   5 Not many books have been _____ by children. (write)

   6 After we had _____ our tea we walked to the lake, which was _____ over. (eat, freeze)

   7 The nest had _____ to the ground but the young had _____ away. (fall, fly)

   8 Our school was _____ by Leigh and Woodvale had _____ to Neston. (beat, lose)

   9 Our kittens have _____ a lot since they were _____ on milk and fish. (grow, feed)

   10 I have _____ the grass and Asif has _____ the edges of the lawn. (mow, trim)

Homonyms

A   Here are illustrated eight pairs of common nouns. Each pair is often confused because they sound the same.

Write out what each pair is. The first one is done for you.

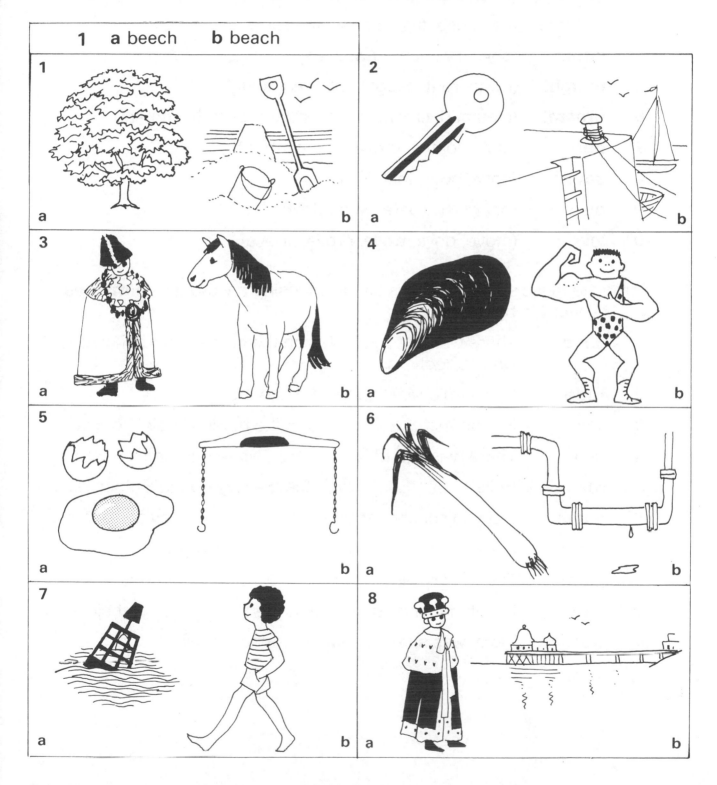

1   **a** beech   **b** beach

B   Now write sentences for each of the nouns.

Rhyming words

A Which words in brackets **rhyme** with the word in bold type?

1 **touch** (pouch, much, rush, coach, such)

2 **gnaw** (gnu, knee, gnarl, raw, gnat)

3 **(to) use** (us, loose, fuse, noose, puss)

4 **know** (cow, now, low, sew, shoe)

5 **nought** (route, rout, caught, laughed, sought)

6 **dreamt** (gleamed, creamed, unkempt, steamed, cement)

7 **both** (cloth, loathe, growth, botch, booth)

8 **soul** (howl, bowl, foul, fowl, foal)

9 **clear** (bear, near, dare, wear, deer)

10 **love** (move, dove, wove, drove, above)

B Complete these sentences sensibly by choosing a word which **rhymes** with the word in bold type.

1 **cane** There was a _____ on the carpet where the coffee was spilled.

2 **rude** I am afraid Mr Rigby is in a very bad _____ .

3 **vain** Pull on the _____ and the horse will slow down.

4 **fear** There was a loud _____ when our team scored.

5 **rot** Bella's _____ won the 'Sailing Round Britain' race.

6 **haste** Did you see the rabbit being _____ by the dog?

7 **sea** I'm sorry but I do not _____ with you.

8 **glum** The hungry birds ate every _____ of bread.

9 **know** In autumn and spring the farmers _____ their seed.

10 **worse** Vicky was sure she put her money in her _____ .

Prepositions

Write a sentence about each picture and underline the **preposition**.

The list will help you.

The first one could be: The police officer dives into the river.

across	behind	amongst	through	off	up	into	above
between	under	after	over	against	on	by	

Direct speech (1)

A   Copy out the words which are actually **spoken** in the following sentences.

1   "Where are my slippers?" asked Dad.

2   "Come to my house on Saturday morning," said Oliver.

3   The teacher looked at her watch and said, "You're late."

4   "Yes," answered the boy, counting his money carefully.

5   "Paul said he was very hungry," said Aled.

6   "Stop looking !" shouted Roger, "I've found it."

7   "Washington is the capital of the USA," replied Malcolm.

8   "Penalty!" roared the crowd, as their striker was tripped in the penalty area.

9   "Good morning," the milkman said. "You're up early."

10   "Try to write an interesting story, Jenny," said Mrs Smith.

11   "Today has been a happy day," shouted Ian. "Not for me though," replied Ann, "I've lost my purse."

12   "I was asleep," cried Fatima. "The thunder woke me up. I'm frightened. Please come and talk to me."

B   Write sentences containing **direct speech** "..........................." about each of the following:

1   something you said to your teacher

2   something you asked the police officer

3   something you whispered to your friend

4   something you shouted to your dog

5   something your teacher told you to do

6   something you asked your dad or mum

Verbs (3)

A   Complete these sentences by choosing suitable **verbs** to fit in the spaces.

1   Hillary and Tenzing .... Everest in 1953.

2   Captain Webb .... the English Channel in 1875.

3   In 1954 Roger Bannister .... the mile in under four minutes.

4   Neil Armstrong and Edwin Aldrin .... on the moon in 1969.

5   The joiner .... a hole through the piece of wood.

6   The thief .... with a large sum of money.

7   The leaves of the tree .... in the breeze.

8   The judge .... sentence on the guilty man.

9   Mark .... a hat-trick for the school team.

10   The lorry .... on the greasy road and hit a wall.

11   The house was unsafe so it was ....

12   Smoking is .... in all enclosed public places.

B   Write the **verbs**.

1   u n __ __ __ __   to take the cover off a parcel

2   l __ __ __ __   to get to know something; to study

3   h __ __ __ __   to go quickly

4   d __ __ __ __ __ y   to ruin completely

5   s __ __ __ __   to slip along something smooth, such as ice

6   r __ __ __ __ __   to save someone or something from danger

7   s c __ __ __ __ __   to throw things around in all directions

8   g __ __ __ __   to look after; to keep safe

9   r __ __ __ __ __   to say or do again

10   w r __ __ __ __ __   to move by twisting and turning

Better words

A   Rewrite these sentences using a better word than **got**.

   1   The window cleaner **got** down the ladder very quickly.

   2   By using a file they **got** out of prison.

   3   I **got** a nice present on my birthday.

   4   "At last he's **got** what I'm trying to explain to him," said the teacher.

   5   John has **got** many stamps since he started the hobby.

   6   Shazia **got** her homework finished quite early.

   7   Since school closed for summer, he's **got** very silly.

   8   Michael has **got** the puppy upstairs.

B   Rewrite these sentences using a better word than **nice**.

   1   Skiing is such a **nice** experience.

   2   My medicine has not got a very **nice** taste.

   3   We saw a **nice** film about diving for treasure.

   4   Those strawberry cream tarts were **nice**.

   5   It's a change to see you looking so **nice**.

   6   Kim is a **nice** dog, and in no way is she silly.

   7   I hope the weather is **nice** so that we can sit on the beach.

   8   After finishing the cross country we had a **nice** drink of orange.

C   Rewrite these sentences using a better word than **said**.

   1   "Am I on the right road for Marlborough?" **said** the driver.

   2   "Be careful! The roof is going to fall in,' **said** the police officer.

   3   Omar moved close to Tom and **said**, "Keep this a secret."

   4   "I think you would be better to make another one," **said** Mum.

   5   The injured girl lay still on the playground. "My leg hurts," she **said**.

   6   At assembly the headmistress **said** that we could all watch the sports.

   7   "Give me one more chance," **said** the prisoner.

   8   "You cannot park your car here," **said** the traffic warden.

Adverbs(2)

A Complete these sentences by adding suitable **adverbs**.

1 The lifeguard swam .... as there was no time to lose.

2 The firefighter struggled .... but he could not reach the trapped man.

3 The thrush sang .... as it perched on the garden fence.

4 The guard dog barked .... as the two men went towards the gate.

5 Brian and Billy played .... and woke up the baby.

6 The rain fell .... so we all ran under the tree.

7 The aeroplane landed .... in spite of the fog.

8 Everyone laughed .... when they watched the clowns.

9 Parveen worked her sums .... and finished ....

10 I bumped into the old man .... as he turned .... into the street.

11 The storm arose .... , and we rowed .... for the shore.

12 The angry bull rushed .... at the boys who had to climb .... up the oak tree.

B Use the following pairs of words, **verbs** and **adverbs**, in sentences of your own.

1	limped slowly	7	talked quietly
2	crashed heavily	8	swam strongly
3	marched smartly	9	cried frantically
4	shone brightly	10	laughed merrily
5	argued noisily	11	listened patiently
6	discovered accidentally	12	increased rapidly

Collective nouns

A   Write suitable **collective nouns** for the following.

1 an _____ of soldiers   6 a _____ of stairs

2 a _____ of books   7 a _____ of furniture

3 a _____ of insects   8 a _____ of stamps

4 a _____ of teachers   9 an _____ of poems

5 a _____ of wolves   10 a _____ of whales

B   What would you expect people to be doing in the groups named below?

1   a choir   5   an orchestra

2   a crew   6   a team

3   a party   7   a queue

4   a mob   8   a troupe

C   There are six pictures below. Each can be described by a **plural** noun or by a **collective** noun. Name each picture in both ways. The first one is done for you.

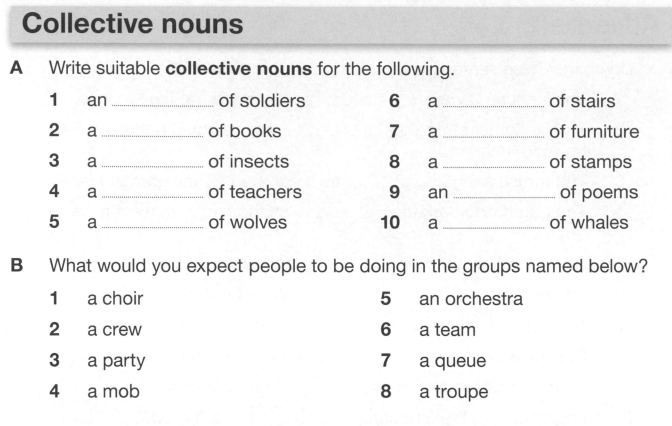

1 puppies—litter

Mixed bag (2)

A   Complete these sentences by using **past** or **passed**.

   1   Dai _____ his driving test.

   2   The boy ran _____ our door.

   3   History is the study of the _____ .

   4   The time _____ quickly at the football match.

   5   The racing cars sped _____ the pits.

   6   Gary _____ the ball through the hoop.

   7   Heavy rain during the _____ week caused flooding.

   8   For the _____ year John and Sophie have been in Miss Green's class.

   9   Fiona tiptoed _____ the sleeping dog.

  10   Old people talk about the _____ rather than the present or future.

B   Complete the sentences by choosing the correct word from the brackets.

   1   Day is to sun as night is to (dark, stars, moon).

   2   Fur is to rabbit as feathers are to (fox, animal, owl, cage).

   3   Hat is to head as sock is to (shoe, foot, arm, hand).

   4   Door is to wood as coat is to (hat, gloves, cloth, trousers).

   5   Young is to old as early is to (baby, now, late, child).

   6   Calf is to cow as puppy is to (cat, bull, playful, dog).

C   Complete these sentences by choosing the correct word from the brackets.

   1   Darren has (fell, fall, fallen) down the stairs.

   2   Anybody (is, are) allowed to borrow a book.

   3   He was (laying, lying, laid) on the town hall lawn.

   4   They have (sang, sung, singed) that song at our concert.

   5   Susan had (ate, eaten, eat) all her sweets.

   6   The teacher has (spoke, speak, spoken) to Nicola about it.

   7   Tom ran quickly to the station but he (mist, missed) the train.

   8   Nobody has (never, ever) climbed that mountain.

   9   The boy hasn't (nothing, anything) to do with it.

  10   My dad is (learning, teaching) me to play chess.

Pronouns

A   Write out the **pronouns** in the following sentences.

    1   Paul's uncle took him to watch the FA cup final.

    2   Heather reminded me that she should go swimming.

    3   They told us that we must not swim in the river.

    4   We always liked to listen to him telling jokes.

    5   Mark told Dawn that he would take her to the cinema.

    6   Would you like to speak to them now?

    7   The pilot told them they would be landing soon.

    8   You must be careful when you use his air rifle.

    9   The dog hid his bone but forgot where it was hidden!

   10   The teacher always allows us to take our books home.

B   Write out these sentences and put a **pronoun** from the list in place of the words in bold type.

they	us	he	it	him	she	them	her

    1   Wait for **David** in the park.

    2   **Sally** gave **Jessica** a birthday present.

    3   Why doesn't **Mr Ahmed** give **Mr Perkins** the book?

    4   **Mrs Bladen and Mrs Makin** cannot find **the letter**.

    5   **Caroline** is not going with **Tom, Heather and Syed**.

    6   Pick **the flowers** and take some to **Mrs Holmes**.

    7   **Nasreen** cannot take **Helena** because **John** has the car.

    8   **Mr Thomas** told **John** to put **the hamsters** back in the cage.

    9   **Danny and Patrick** met **Emily**.

   10   **Jake** met **David and me**.

Similes

A   This list of words will help you to write out the **similes** connected with the following pictures of animals.

> agile   graceful   busy   wise   brave   cunning   slippery   slow

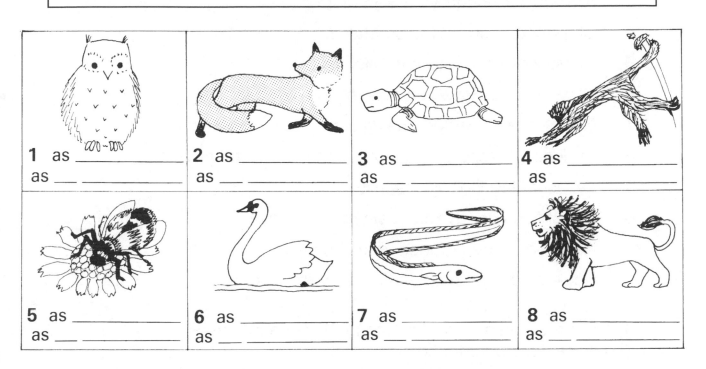

1 as _____
as ___ _____

2 as _____
as ___ _____

3 as _____
as ___ _____

4 as _____
as ___ _____

5 as _____
as ___ _____

6 as _____
as ___ _____

7 as _____
as ___ _____

8 as _____
as ___ _____

B   Complete these **similes** by choosing the best word in the brackets.

1   as blind as a (chicken, deer, rabbit, bat)

2   as flat as a (kettle, loaf, pancake, saucer)

3   as timid as a (lion, mouse, giant, mule)

4   as proud as a (rabbit, mouse, peacock, wolf)

5   as happy as a (lark, pig, daisy, serpent)

6   as thin as a (house, football, rake, king)

C   Complete these **similes** by adding suitable words.

1   as tough as _____   7   as _____ as a new pin

2   as dry as _____   8   as _____ as two peas in a pod

3   as good as _____   9   as _____ as a cucumber

4   as keen as _____   10 as _____ as coal

5   as sweet as _____   11 as _____ as toast

6   as cold as _____   12 as _____ as clockwork

Direct speech (2)

A   Write out these sentences putting in the speech marks "............................".

    1   I am going home, said Mark.

    2   Bring my books, please, said Mr Mills.

    3   Are you very hungry? asked Mum.

    4   Stop that! shouted the caretaker.

    5   Be very quiet, whispered Michael.

    6   David asked, Have you seen my cricket bat?

    7   Please close the door, he said. Someone may hear us.

    8   Suddenly I stopped. I've forgotten my ticket, I said.

    9   Yes, shouted Bobby. It's mine.

  10   It isn't fair, I cried. You cheated.

  11   Hazel said, Aren't those roses beautiful?

  12   Rosie said she couldn't stay, explained Leah.

B   Write out these sentences putting in the speech marks "............................" and other necessary punctuation.

    1   That doesn't belong to me said Angus.

    2   Have you seen my dog Cathy asked.

    3   Try that coat on suggested the shop assistant.

    4   The old man looked very angry get out he yelled.

    5   That's not hard he boasted watch me do it.

    6   No Andrew the coach said you are not shooting first time.

    7   Alex asked me to watch him Stuart explained.

    8   Will you please carry this parcel for me asked the old lady.

    9   Where have you been I've been waiting an hour for you grumbled Rashid.

  10   The answer Mr Davis gave me was you can't come in with your shoes on.

Conjunctions

A   Write out the **conjunctions** in each of these sentences.

1   The children played on the beach and went in the sea.

2   The cricket match was abandoned because it was raining.

3   We are moving to London if Dad can get a job.

4   You must have a ticket otherwise you won't get in.

5   Let's wait here until the bus comes.

6   Ian is not sure whether he can come with us.

7   We pulled at the door, but could not open it.

8   You need not stay unless you wish to.

9   Most people feel nervous when they visit the dentist.

10   Heather sprained her ankle so she cannot go to school.

B   Use one of the **conjunctions** from the list to complete each of the sentences.

> **because   and   when   for   but   although**
> **untll   since   wherever   while**

1   I am disappointed with her .... she should know better.

2   We have been here .... you left.

3   My knee is still swollen .... I have rested it.

4   The faithful sheepdog followed the shepherd .... he went.

5   Bob could not play football .... he had sprained his ankle.

6   You clean the car .... I walk the dog.

7   I was walking to the shops .... I saw the accident.

8   We watched the strange object in the sky .... wc could see it no longer.

9   The sun shone again .... the cricket match continued.

10   Jamie took the penalty for a second time .... he missed again.

Vocabulary and spelling (2)

A Every word begins with **p.** Each pair in the bracket sounds alike. Write out the words.

1
- when you have toothache you have ....
- a sheet of glass in a window ....

2
- colourless, faded, light ....
- a bucket ....

3
- animals' feet with claws ....
- to stop what you are doing for a moment ....

4
- a flat fish which is good to eat ....
- somewhere; a spot or position ....

B Every word begins with **r.** Each pair in the bracket sounds alike.

1
- the underground part of a plant ....
- a road or path from one place to another ....

2
- lines of people or things ....
- a beautiful flower with a thorny stem ....

3
- to lift up ....
- beams of light ....

4
- you must be able to .... to answer this ....
- a tall grass growing near water ....

C Every word begins with **s.** Each pair in the bracket sounds alike.

1
- a male child ....
- the star that gives us heat and light ....

2
- without a curve or a bend ....
- a narrow channel of sea ....

3
- to plant seeds ....
- to use a needle and thread ....

4
- a fence with a step on each side ....
- the manner in which you do something ....

Mixed bag (3)

A Rewrite these sentences using **one word** in place of the words in bold type.

1   Elizabeth **kept out of the way of** Sally and Emma.

2   The window was broken **quite by accident**.

3   During the **great shortage of rain** the pond dried up.

4   My teacher told me that my work was **getting better**.

5   My friend is always **fair and truthful**.

6   At the sale the prices were **made less than before**.

7   The actor was **not able to be heard** at the back of the theatre.

8   Sarah's job at the supermarket is only **for the time being**.

9   Javed told me **over and over again** about his new bicycle.

10 The man dived into the canal **without waiting a second**.

B What do you call the place where

1   doctors see their patients?   s...............................

2   birds are kept?   a...............................

3   chickens are hatched?   i...............................

4   films are shown?   c...............................

5   TV programmes and films are produced?   s...............................

C Write the class name for each of these groups, then add an example of your own.

1   guitar, piano, drums, organ

2   turkey, beef, lamb, chicken

3   squash, golf, football, cricket

4   yacht, trawler, tug, schooner

5   labrador, corgi, terrier, poodle

6   Mercury, Jupiter, Venus, Mars

7   green, orange, red, yellow

8   beech, ash, oak, sycamore

9   sweater, jeans, t-shirt, skirt

10 table, settee, bed, chair

Occupations

A Write the names of the occupations shown in the pictures.

B Name the occupations of the people who sell:

1 writing paper, envelopes, greeting cards.

2 papers and magazines.

3 roses, lillies and carnations.

4 medicines, ointments, cosmetics.

5 precious stones, rings, watches.

6 lamb, beef, venison, turkey.

7 plaice, cod, mackerel, shrimps.

8 pies, cakes, bread, tarts.

C Name the occupation of the person who:

1 looks after zoo animals.

2 grows flowers, shrubs and trees.

3 writes novels.

4 sells goods to the highest bidder.

5 repairs motor cars, motor cycles, etc.

6 cuts, colours and styles hair.

7 carves statues.

8 treats corns and nails on the feet.

Apostrophe – possession

A   Write the following using the apostrophe to show there is **one owner**.

1   the pencil belonging to Peter
2   the gun belonging to the soldier
3   the brush of the caretaker
4   the fields of the farmer
5   the spade belonging to
    Mr Clark

6   the neck of the giraffe
7   the computer belonging to
    the designer
8   the dinner of the dog
9   the feet of the duck
10 the pen belonging to Sally

B   Write the following using the apostrophe to show that there is **more than one owner**.

1   the tents of the scouts
2   the trunks of the elephants
3   the petals belonging to the flowers
4   the submarine of the sailors
5   the room belonging to the
    teachers

6   the boots belonging to the
    footballers
7   the rocket of the astronauts
8   the wings of the birds
9   the club for pilots
10 a school for dancers

C   Write the following using the apostrophe to show that there is **more than one owner**.

1   the helmets of the firefighters
2   the radios belonging to the
    police officers
3   the dresses of the ladies
4   the clothes belonging to the
    babies
5   the gardens of the neighbours

6   the hideout of the thieves
7   the play area for children
8   the sister of the brothers
9   the animals owned by the zoos
10 the horns belonging to the
    oxen

D   Use the apostrophe to show ownership.

1   the fleeces belonging to
    the sheep
2   the ears of the donkey
3   the masks of the divers

4   the feathers of the bird
5   the club belonging to the women
6   the wings belonging to the
    geese

Vocabulary and spelling (3)

A   The answers to these clues all end in **cious**.

   1   very valuable __ __ __ c i o u s

   2   most pleasant to eat __ __ __ __ c i o u s

   3   plenty of room __ __ __ c i o u s

   4   doubting whether something is true __ __ __ __ __ c i o u s

   5   not knowing what is going on around you __ __ __ __ __ __ c i o u s

B   The answers all have **ll** in them.

   1   precious stones, gold, rings   j...........................

   2   10 make a centimetre   m...........................

   3   grub from which a butterfly or moth comes   c...........................

   4   piece of land used as an extra garden   a...........................

   5   the same distance apart all along   p...........................

C   These answers all end in **ible.**

   1   cannot be done   i...........................

   2   unable to be seen   i...........................

   3   showing good sense; wise   s...........................

   4   can be reversed   r...........................

   5   Who is   r........................... for this excellent work?

D   These answers all begin with **ch**.

   1   the 25th of December   Ch...........................

   2   a person who is paid to drive a car   ch...........................

   3   a large tree; its nut is called a conker   ch...........................

   4   a stage in the life of an insect   ch...........................

   5   someone who treats feet   ch...........................

Punctuation

A Rewrite these sentences, using **capital letters** where necessary.

1 tom played squash with terry on monday night.

2 when marie visited london she went in the houses of parliament.

3 every christmas peter stays with his aunty edna in nairobi.

4 britain could import jamaican sugar, new zealand apples and australian wool.

5 the busy holiday months in england are july and august.

6 pelé, the famous footballer, played for santos f.c. in brazil and new york cosmos.

7 chloe's sister, emma, is studying french at sydney university.

8 in 2012 queen elizabeth II celebrated her diamond jubilee.

B Write out these sentences putting in **commas**, **full stops**, **question marks** and **exclamation marks** where necessary.

1 Morag Sally and I went for a walk

2 The cyclist after a brief stop for food resumed the race

3 "If you see him will you ask him to write"

4 Some common metals are bronze lead iron and zinc

5 Grandad after a big dinner went to sleep

6 "Quick march" yelled the drill-sergeant

7 "Are you feeling better today" asked the teacher

8 "What do you think you are doing" shouted the angry farmer

C Write in full these abbreviated words.

1	he'll	3	couldn't	5	I'm	7	they've
2	she's	4	won't	6	you're	8	who's

D Write these words in abbreviated form.

1	they are	3	she cannot	5	he shall not	7	they will
2	you would	4	that is	6	where is	8	where have

Mixed bag (4)

A   Give the meanings of these **abbreviations**.

1	PTO	5	lbw	9	m	13	VIP
2	PC	6	Ave.	10	kph	14	EU
3	Feb.	7	a.m.	11	e.g.	15	cm
4	RSPCA	8	GMT	12	etc.		

B   Write the missing **proper adjectives**.

1   cars made in Britain .... cars

2   apples grown in Canada .... apples

3   peaches from Australia .... peaches

4   bananas grown in Jamaica .... bananas

5   coffee from Kenya .... coffee

6   bacon from Denmark .... bacon

7   watches made in Switzerland .... watches

8   timber from Finland .... timber

9   bulbs from Holland .... bulbs

C   Write the **sound** words.

1   the .... of brakes

2   the .... of rusty hinges

3   the .... of an explosion

4   the .... of a drum

5   the .... of leaves

6   the .... of thunder

D   Write the animal **sounds**.

1   frogs ....

2   owls ....

3   dogs ....

4   cows ....

5   horses ....

6   sheep ....

7   monkeys ....

8   cats ....

Vocabulary – similar meanings

A Choose one of the words in the list in place of a word or words in bold type in the sentences below.

pester	vivid	errors	dilute	various	constantly
exterior	vacant	request	extinguish	surrender	glorious

1   The machine worked **without stopping** for twenty hours.

2   You should **water down** the orange juice.

3   The firefighters worked hard to **put out** the flames.

4   The painters have nearly finished the **outside** of our house.

5   "Don't **bother** me now. I'm too busy," said Francis.

6   You must **apply for** permission to alter your house.

7   There are **assorted** kinds of sweets in the tin.

9   What a **splendid** display of roses!

10 The brave soldiers were determined not to **give themselves up**.

11 Tom used **very bright** colours in his paintings.

12 The old house was **unoccupied** for years.

13 You have made too many **mistakes** in your work.

B Here are twenty-four words which you can arrange into twelve pairs. The words of each pair will have similar meanings.

Use your dictionary to help you to write them in pairs.

pull	guard	floating	crush
grind	polite	disappear	feeble
defend	amaze	haul	genuine
useless	buoyant	sincere	force
weak	compel	support	futile
encourage	courteous	astound	vanish

Singular and plural

A Write these sentences in the **plural** form.

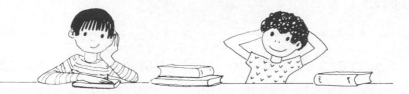

1   The boy has read his book.

2   I am going near Oban for my holiday.

3   The footballer wears a red jersey.

4   I shall sell it to the girl.

5   The girl tripped over the stone and hurt herself.

6   The play wasn't very well acted.

7   I must help to feed the monkey.

8   The man was very tired after he had worked hard in the garden.

9   I saw a goose in the field.

10   This boy wants to play chess.

B Write these sentences in the **singular** form.

1   Our friends came on holiday with us.

2   The police officers checked their watches before they set off.

3   The knives have been sharpened.

4   Some women shouted at us.

5   Firefighters wear uniforms.

6   "Have you seen them?" we asked.

7   Chimpanzees are very intelligent animals.

8   The first chapters of the books were missing.

9   We are sure you do not understand these ideas.

10   We were pleased with the examination results which were published in the papers yesterday.

Adverbs (3)

A Complete these sentences by using **verbs** and **adverbs** so that the second sentence has the same meaning as the first. The first one is done for you.

1 My friend is a careful driver.   My friend drives carefully.

2 Joan gave a quick answer.   Joan _____ .

3 We are all sound sleepers.   We _____ .

4 Sam is a slow reader.   Sam _____ .

5 The other team were bad losers.   The other team _____ .

6 The bright sun shines on the beach.   The sun _____ .

7 The explorer made an interesting speech.   The explorer _____ .

8 Darren is a strong swimmer.   Darren _____ .

9 The secretary sent a prompt answer.   The secretary _____ .

10 Rob was a skilful player.   Rob _____ .

B Rewrite these sentences, by using **one adverb** in place of the words in heavy type.

1 The monk copied the manuscript **with great care**.

2 The electric cables were not joined **in the correct way**.

3 Sensible people visit their dentist **at regular times**.

4 The burglar entered the house **without making a sound**.

5 The two space ships docked **exactly on time**.

6 The kind man gave **a lot of money** to the charity.

7 Jasmine asked the question **in a polite way**.

8 **In the end** the battered ship managed to reach land.

9 The artist looked **with pride** at his latest painting.

10 James worked out all the problems **in his head**.

Comprehension (1)

AVALANCHE

Brachen was crammed to overflowing. Travellers from the long-distance trains held up by the snowfall filled the hotels. Evacuees from the threatened mountain villages were billeted on private families. The large waiting rooms next to the station restaurant had been cleared to receive refugees. The proprietor of the restaurant, who normally did a thriving business, had handed over his kitchen and his coffee machines to the Red Cross and his staff were working as volunteers.

The wireless had been moved to the left luggage department, where it was kept turned on all day, so that anyone who wanted to could listen to the latest reports on what was happening in the threatened districts.

In the early morning light the long platform stretched away, lonely and deserted. No express trains stopped there now for a few bustling minutes before speeding away again. Everything looked grey: the rails, the dirty snow, the trucks in the siding and the long green Lucerne–Rome express, which had been standing for eight hours and thirty-two minutes, waiting for the signal to move.

A few railwaymen in blue overalls and black caps moved about. Now and then the sound of lowing came from one of the cattle trucks that stood in a siding under the broad station roof. The heads of three white oxen with great dewlaps gazed out mildly through an opening. The heavy snow-ploughs stood in another siding. Two soldiers in overalls were working on them.

At seven the wireless began to give the first news bulletins. A little group of evacuees and three of the station officials gathered in front of the left luggage office. People with pale sleepy faces climbed down out of the waiting train and joined them.

The Pestalozzi boys straggled out of the warm, stuffy waiting room into the clear, frosty morning outside. Paolo, with his black curls standing on end, was yawning his head off. As soon as they saw the group on the platform and heard the familiar voice of the announcer, they came rushing along to listen. All except Werner, who trailed along behind them with his hands in his pockets and a reluctant expression on his face.

From *Avalanche* by A. Rutgers Van Der Loeff

1 Give two reasons why Brachen was filled to overflowing.

2 Name the two cities the green express connected.

3 What was the time of the first news bulletin?

4 Why weren't any express trains calling at Brachen?

5 What uniform was worn by the railwaymen?

6 Describe the weather that particular morning.

7 Name two kinds of railway equipment kept round the station.

8 Give two reasons why the proprietor of the restaurant was a 'good' man.

9 Why was the wireless moved to the left luggage office?

10 How do you know Paolo was half asleep?

11 Where do you think this disaster took place?

12 Find the words in the passage that mean:

a	messages.	e	owner.
b	successful.	f	giving services freely.
c	unwilling.	g	crowded.
d	radio.	h	people moved because of danger.

13 For you to find out:

a Who began the Red Cross? When? Where? Why?

b What are Pestalozzi Children's Villages?

c What are dewlaps?

Adjectives (2)

Complete the following sentences using **adjectives** formed from the nouns in the brackets.

A 1 The children were _____ after playing in the hot sun. (thirst)

   2 Grandad was very _____ after weeding the garden. (sleep)

   3 The small boat was tossed about in the _____ sea. (storm)

   4 The cricket match was spoiled because of the _____ weather.   (shower)

B 1 The _____ water will kill the fish.   (ice)

   2 Let's sit in this _____ part of the park.   (shade)

   3 It's too _____ to see the yachts in the bay.   (haze)

   4 The cactus is a _____ plant.   (prickle)

C 1 Have you read Paula's _____ poem?   (fun)

   2 I'm not walking along that _____ path.   (mud)

   3 The chinchilla is a _____ animal.   (fur)

   4 Your recorder makes a _____ noise.   (tin)

D 1 Look at that _____ puppy.   (mischief)

   2 My friend is a _____ footballer.   (skill)

   3 Mrs Long wears _____ jewellery.   (expense)

   4 A firefighter has a _____ job.   (danger)

E Form **adjectives** from the following nouns.

1	haste	6	poison	11	nature
2	leak	7	circle	12	expense
3	skin	8	juice	13	sun
4	wool	9	accident	14	sympathy
5	anger	10	death	15	depth

A   One word for several

Rewrite the following sentences, replacing the words in bold type with one word.

1   The **people who lived next door** were very helpful when Mum was ill.

2   Tom kept his model railway in the **room where he slept**.

3   Shafilea walked along the corridor **without making a noise**.

4   At the airport our family joined the long **line of waiting people**.

5   My **mother's brother** often comes fishing with us.

6   The teacher said she had not **made up her mind** whether to have the match.

7   Jess said that she had started to write her **own life story**.

8   Our electric meter is read **once every three months**.

9   There was a **general shortage of food** after the earthquake.

10   If you heat a piece of steel it will **get bigger**.

B   Incorrect sentences

Rewrite the following sentences correctly.

1   Jamie played football with Peter and I.

2   Mr Peacock is headmaster of a girl's school.

3   The cat was run over with a car.

4   Look at the baby drinking from it's bottle.

5   Alan, Bob and Bill was sheltering from the storm.

6   I have earned less house marks this term.

7   "I didn't do nothing wrong," sobbed Mark.

8   Our teacher said he would learn me to dive in the pool.

9   Frank is tallest than the other two boys.

10   None of the pencils are sharp.

Nouns and verbs – formation

A Complete these sentences by filling in the blanks with **verbs** formed from the nouns in brackets.

1 The results of the art competition were _____ at assembly. (announcement)

2 They _____ to choose a new goalkeeper. (decision)

3 Every swimmer _____ the skill of Mark. (admiration)

4 Dr Livingstone _____ the Victoria Falls in Africa. (discovery)

5 We were _____ to learn that the fishermen were safe. (relief)

6 The elephants were _____ by the keeper. (food)

7 I hope the divers _____ the lost treasure ship. (discovery)

8 Jane said she would _____ ten friends to her party. (invitation)

9 When we have more rain the grass will _____ . (growth)

10 You will _____ more if you read more. (knowledge)

B Complete these sentences by filling in the blanks with **nouns** formed from the verbs in brackets.

1 Crowds greeted the _____ of the pop star. (arrive)

2 The children's _____ at the concert was excellent. (behave)

3 The _____ was blocked by fallen bricks. (enter)

4 Grace suffered a painful _____ when she fell on the ice. (injure)

5 The audience applauded the _____ of the orchestra. (perform)

6 We had a large _____ of groceries. (deliver)

7 We were five kilometres away but heard the _____ . (explode)

8 The general expected _____ from all his soldiers. (obey)

9 Professor Brytor's _____ will help farmers. (invent)

10 The referee's _____ is always final. (decide)

Mixed bag (5)

A   Odd one out

Write out the word in each group which does not fit in with the others.

1   talk, listen, say, tell, speak, utter, remark

2   aged, antique, modern, elderly, ancient, old

3   home, flat, residence, dwelling, school, house

4   fast, quick, rapid, early, swift, speedy

5   small, tiny, minute, little, hole, wee, puny

6   great, huge, vast, immense, square, enormous

7   bold, fearless, cautious, adventurous, daring

8   tutor, scholar, student, pupil, learner

9   dark, gloomy, dismal, dreary, deadly, sombre

10   collect, gather, assemble, amass, accumulate, scatter

11   seize, loosen, grasp, clutch, clasp, clench

12   dash, rush, hurry, loiter, scurry, scoot

B   Opposites

Write the opposites of the following words.

1	cowardly	4	thoughtless	7	horizontal
2	regular	5	gentle	8	reckless
3	gigantic	6	peculiar	9	abundant

C   Rhyming words

Write out the word that rhymes with the word in bold type.

1	**plate**	meat	plait	weight	pleat
2	**sane**	scene	rein	wine	green
3	**fetch**	bleach	batch	clutch	stretch
4	**foul**	fool	howl	bowl	four
5	**port**	pour	part	court	hurt
6	**suite**	suit	sure	soot	beat
7	**field**	healed	felled	fooled	farmed
8	**meant**	mean	stint	tent	meal

Vocabulary and spelling (4)

A   The answers to these clues have either **ei** or **ie** in them.

    1   the daughter of your brother or sister   n __ __ __ __

    2   a piece of cloth for wiping your nose
       h __ __ __ __ __ __ __ __ __ __

    3   the roof of a room   c __ __ __ __ __ __

    4   someone who steals   t __ __ __ __

    5   to think that something is true   b __ __ __ __ __ __

    6   to have something given to you   r __ __ __ __ __ __

    7   part of something   p __ __ __ __

    8   someone you like; a pal   f __ __ __ __ __

    9   to mislead or cheat   d __ __ __ __ __ __

    10   how tall a thing is   h __ __ __ __ __

B   These answers all have **y** in them.

    1   a machine for making electricity   d..

    2   a sweet-smelling spring flower   h..

    3   an African wild animal like a dog   h..

    4   a high explosive   d..

    5   a very large snake   p..

C   These answers all end in **or**.

    1   an imaginary line around the Earth's centre .... or

    2   a moving staircase .... or

    3   someone who writes a book .... or

    4   someone who watches a game, a show, etc. .... or

    5   a passage-way .... or

Direct and indirect speech

A Change these sentences to **indirect speech**.

Look at this example.

Dad said, "We'll miss the bus."   (direct speech)

Dad said that we would miss the bus.   (indirect speech)

1   Brian said, "I'm tired after that long walk."

2   The caretaker said, "I've lost my big brush".

3   "I've lost my keys," said the teacher.

4   "Has anyone found a bunch of keys?" asked the teacher.

5   "You can stay a little longer," suggested Eric.

6   "Try harder," my dad advised, "or you'll never finish the job."

7   "Have you seen a black and white kitten?" the old lady asked.

8   "You musn't play near the river, Billy," warned his friend.

9   He said, "I used to play for the first team."

10   "I am sure," said Mr Thomas, "that you haven't listened."

B Change these sentences from indirect to **direct speech**.

e.g. The girl said she was tired.   (indirect)

The girl said, "I am tired."   (direct)

1   The boys said they were very sorry for being late.

2   Mum said that dinner was ready.

3   The pilot remarked that it may be a bumpy flight.

4   Tom said that he would not be able to play.

5   Dora asked if I was going to town.

6   The secretary said that the paper was hers.

7   The teacher said that she wouldn't be away long.

8   The farmer explained that he was going to dig some drains.

9   The boy asked Mr Aitken if he would return his football.

10   I asked Mr Perkins where he would be going in August.

Comprehension (2)

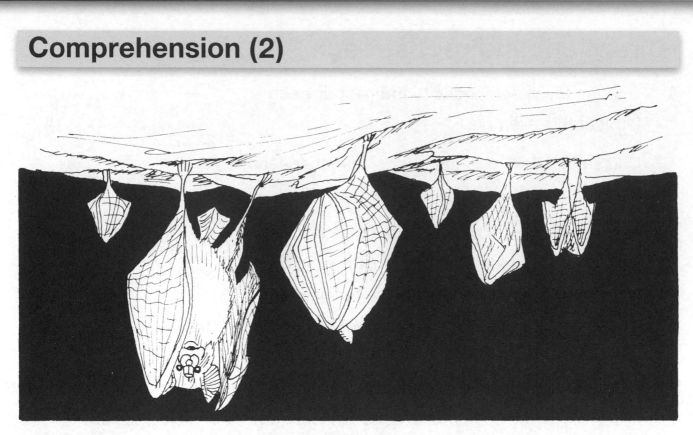

BATS

I had reached a deep ravine in the great limestone rocks of Somerset. There are dozens of caverns and most of them afford a shelter for bats of six or seven different species. Horseshoe Bats are abundant. Like the huge chrysalids of some exotic butterfly, they hang from the walls of the caverns, still, silent, and torpid. But shine an electric torch on their dusky bodies or breathe ever so lightly on them and they flex their legs and draw themselves up tightly to the rock. They are profoundly asleep.

In these caverns lives the handsome Natterer's Bat, a pretty creature with long, almost transparent ears. Its underside is a soft white, very noticeable when the bat is on the wing. In fact among some country-folk this species has been dubbed the "White-waistcoat Bat". Another species, known as the Whiskered Bat, also inhabits the same caves. It has a goblin-like expression and its fur is grizzled chestnut above and dusky beneath. Both these bats are difficult to capture, for they wedge themselves deep in the crevices.

With luck a Long-eared Bat may be found here. Its enormous ears are as long as its body. Its piteous eyes stand out like beads. Why has this species got such long ears? Perhaps because it hunts at night when insects are scarce.

The rarest of the bats inhabiting these caves is the Barbastelle. One April I could plainly see one with its curiously formed ears, its evil-looking face and black shining eyes, as my electric torch revealed it in the depths of a narrow crevice. For a few minutes it defied me from its fastness, squeaking in a querulous manner. Finally it crept out of sight, crying its protest until its voice faded away into a deep, metallic buzz.

By J.W. Robertson Scott, from *The Countryman Book*, the Hamlyn Publishing Group Ltd. (originally published by Odhams Press Ltd.)

1   Give the names of all the different kinds of bats found by the writer.

2   Which was the most common bat he found?

3   Which bats were the most difficult to capture? Why?

4   What do bats feed on ?

5   Describe, in your own words, the type of sleep enjoyed by Horseshoe Bats.

6   Which bat makes a 'metallic buzz' sound?

7   What is the main difference between the appearance of a Whiskered Bat and a Natterer's Bat?

8   What are chrysalids? Why are they compared with bats?

9   Which was the rarest bat found in the caverns?

10 Find the words in the passage that mean:

a	very deeply.	f	named.
b	sort or kind.	g	very sad.
c	not moving.	h	allow permit.
d	made known.	i	very plentiful.
e	lives in.	j	easily seen through.

Mixed bag (6)

Rearrange these groups of letters to make names of the following.

A Zoo animals

1 N O I L	3 E F I G R F A	5 A L E M C
2 O K E M Y N	4 B A Z E R	6 N O A O G R K A

B Vegetables

1 A E P	3 N N O O I	5 N I R T U P
2 O O T T A P	4 O T C R A R	6 A E B B C G A

C Trees

1 S A H	3 N E I P	5 A R C D E
2 K O A	4 E C B H E	6 H S T U C T E N

D Choose the correct **prefix** from the list below to form opposite meanings to these twelve words.

1 correct	5 wrap	9 fortunate
2 possible	6 convenient	10 experienced
3 regular	7 comfortable	11 comfort
4 obedient	8 polite	12 responsible

> ir ....   un ....   dis ....
>
> im ....   in ....

E Rewrite the following sentences by choosing the correct form of the word in brackets.

1 Sheila is the .... swimmer in the school.   (fast)

2 Prince is the .... horse in the race.   (young)

3 Terry is the .... of the three boys.   (strong)

4 The lounge is the .... of the two rooms.   (warm)

5 Our school is .... than Kimwood High.   (large)

6 Do you think Sam is a .... runner than Darren?   (good)

Answers

Page 2 Nouns
A 1 dog, field **2** bananas, custard, dish
3 elephants, logs **4** wine, grapes
5 police officer, cars, lorries **6** children,
teachers, circus **7** lifeguard, swimmer
8 night, Tom, book, walk **9** porridge,
sausages, egg, toast, breakfast
10 helicopter, football field, school
B 1 cuckoo **2** ceiling **3** concrete **4** cider
5 customer **6** cousin **7** crane **8** cheese
9 calendar **10** caterpillar

Page 3 Adjectives (1)
A 1 damp, foggy **2** blind, wooden
3 short, fat, tall, slim **4** large, powerful,
striped **5** small, strong, rough **6** slender,
long, short **7** fast, thrilling, large **8** thick,
blue, red, woollen **9** extinct, flightless,
giant **10** brave, dangerous, hot, humid
B 1 priceless **2** fatal **3** fierce **4** fragrant
5 empty **6** huge **7** courageous
8 victorious **9** difficult **10** nourishing
C Check your child's sentences.

Page 4 Verbs (1)
A 1 slipped, fell **2** finished, returned
3 ate, ran **4** took, make **5** fed, cleaned
6 baked, cleaned, washed **7** saw, rescue
8 sped, braked, skidded **9** climbed,
checked **10** fell, broke
B 1 measured **2** collided **3** swooped
4 perched **5** collapsed **6** flickered
7 shattered **8** repeated **9** interrupted
10 marooned
C Check your child's sentences.

Page 5 Adverbs (1)
A 1 swiftly **2** loudly **3** brightly
4 comfortably **5** annually **6** wearily
7 slowly, quickly **8** clearly **9** suddenly,
cleverly **10** immediately, late
B 1 correctly **2** foolishly **3** soundly

4 frantically **5** fiercely **6** briefly **7** silently
8 anxiously **9** tunefully **10** bitterly
C Check your child's sentences.

Page 6 Alphabetical order
A bicycle, comb, duck, hammer, kite, pig
B 1 beach, cage, hobby, meat, runway,
warrior
2 acorn, grass, nylon, quiz, smell, white
3 cry, duck, frost, jelly, puzzle, vein
C sailor, seesaw, shark, skeleton, spear,
star
D 1 path, pea, pier, potato, prize, public
2 bed, bite, black, boat, bread, bulb
3 wasp, weak, whip, witch, worm, wrist
E cactus, cake, camera, caravan, castle,
catapult
F 1 spade, speak, spin, spoon, spun, spy
2 price, pride, prime, princess, prison, prize
3 chain, chalk, chameleon, channel, chart,
chatter

Page 7 Sentences
A 1 The man is putting his hat **on his head**.
2 Dad is wearing a watch **on his wrist**.
3 Sam is painting **the back door**.
4 It was raining heavily **so Jean put up her
umbrella**.
5 The train is stopping **at the signal**.
6 Nicky is cutting bread **with a knife**.
7 The aeroplane is landing **at Manchester
Airport**.
8 The lifeboat is speeding **to rescue the
sailors**.
B 1–5 Check that your child's chosen
words are suitable.
C 1–5 Check that your child's chosen
words are suitable.

Page 8 Compound words
A 1 head + light = headlight
2 post + card = postcard

3 life + belt = lifebelt
4 air + plane = airplane
5 foot + print = footprint
6 sun + dial = sundial
7 fire + fighter = firefighter
8 hand + cuff = handcuff
9 hedge + hog = hedgehog
10 snow + flake = snowflake
11 bed + room = bedroom
12 wood + pecker = woodpecker
B Check that your child's answers are compound words.

Page 9 Vocabulary and spelling (1)
A ice, cafe, elephant, library, alphabet, nightmare, dandelion = Iceland
B bulldozer, ancient, dodge, glacier, eagle, ranch = badger
C August, pork, rich, infant, customer, octopus, triangle = apricot

Page 10 Singular and plural
1 horse – horses 2 tooth – teeth
3 piano – pianos 4 man – men
5 star – stars 6 foot – feet 7 baby – babies
8 bus – buses 9 monkey – monkeys
10 leaf – leaves 11 volcano – volcanoes
12 sheep – sheep 13 mousetrap – mousetraps 14 oasis – oases 15 tree – trees

Page 11 Mixed bag (1)
A 1 thin 2 close 3 sour 4 inside 5 pretty
6 rude 7 imaginary/fake 8 permanent
9 failure 10 private
B 1–10 Check that your child's words have a similar meaning to those written.
C 1 Football 2 Rugby 3 Netball 4 Cricket
5 Squash 6 Swimming 7 Hockey 8 Tennis
9 Angling 10 Badminton

Page 12 Gender
A 1 grandfather 2 steward 3 peacock
4 manager 5 horse 6 headmaster 7 boar
8 duke 9 monk
B 1 actress 2 hind 3 lady 4 stepmum
5 female 6 filly 7 widow 8 mother-in-law
9 uncle
C 1 wizard/witch 2 waiter/waitress 3 mayor/mayoress 4 groom/bride 5 stag/hind

Page 13 Picture story
Check that your child's story describes what is happening in the pictures.

Page 14 Verbs (2)
Past tense
A 1 shook 2 held 3 sprang 4 struck
5 wrote 6 stopped 7 thought, was 8 drove, found, were 9 went, had 10 bled, fell
Past participle
B 1 known 2 gone 3 swollen 4 hidden
5 written 6 eaten, frozen 7 fallen, flown
8 beaten, lost 9 grown, fed 10 mown, trimmed

Page 15 Homonyms
A 2a key b quay 3a mayor b mare
4a mussel b muscle 5a yolk b yoke 6a leek
b leak 7a buoy b boy 8a peer b pier
B Check that your child's sentences include the nouns given in Question A.

Page 16 Rhyming words
A 1 much, such 2 raw 3 fuse 4 low, sew
5 caught, sought 6 unkempt, cement
7 growth 8 bowl, foal 9 near, deer 10 dove, above
B 1 stain 2 mood 3 rein 4 cheer 5 yacht
6 chased 7 agree 8 crumb 9 sow 10 purse

Page 17 Prepositions
Check that your child's sentences describe the relevant picture and include an appropriate preposition from the box.

Page 18 Direct speech (1)
A 1 Where are my slippers?

2 Come to my house on Saturday morning.
3 You're late.
4 Yes.
5 Paul said he was very hungry.
6 Stop looking....I've found it.
7 Washington is the capital of the USA.
8 Penalty.
9 Good morning....You're up early.
10 Try to write an interesting story, Jenny.
11 Today has been a happy day....Not for me
though....I've lost my purse.
12 I was asleep....The thunder woke me up.
I'm frightened. Please come and talk to me.
B 1–6 Check your child's answers.

Page 19 Verbs (3)
A 1–12 Check that your child has used a
suitable verb to complete the sentences.
B 1 unwrap **2** learn **3** hurry **4** destroy
5 slide **6** rescue **7** scatter **8** guard
9 repeat **10** wriggle

Page 20 Better words
A, B and C Check that your child's chosen
words are suitable for each sentence.

Page 21 Adverbs (2)
A 1–12 Check that your child's chosen
adverbs are suitable for each sentence.
B 1–12 Check that your child's sentences
use the given verbs and adverbs suitably.

Page 22 Collective nouns
A 1 army **2** library **3** swarm **4** staff
5 pack **6** flight **7** suite **8** collection or
album **9** anthology **10** school
B 1 singing **2** working on a ship **3** enjoying
themselves **4** rioting **5** playing music
6 playing a game **7** waiting **8** dancing
C 2 wolves – pack **3** tools – set
4 footballers – team **5** ships – fleet
6 bananas – bunch

Page 23 Mixed bag (2)
A 1 passed **2** past **3** past **4** passed
5 past **6** passed **7** past **8** past **9** past
10 past
B 1 moon **2** owl **3** foot **4** cloth **5** late
6 dog
C 1 fallen **2** is **3** lying **4** sung **5** eaten
6 spoken **7** missed **8** ever **9** anything
10 teaching

Page 24 Pronouns
A 1 him **2** me, she **3** They, us, we **4** We,
him **5** he, her **6** you, them **7** them, they
8 You, you, his **9** his, it **10** us, our
B 1 him **2** she, her **3** he, him **4** they, it
5 she, them **6** them, her **7** she, her, he
8 he, him, them **9** they, her **10** he, us

Page 25 Similes
A 1 as wise as an owl **2** as cunning as a
fox **3** as slow as a tortoise **4** as agile as a
monkey **5** as busy as a bee **6** as graceful as
a swan **7** as slippery as an eel **8** as brave as
a lion
B 1 bat **2** pancake **3** mouse **4** peacock
5 lark **6** rake
C Examples: 1 old boots **2** bone **3** gold
4 mustard **5** honey **6** ice **7** clean **8** alike
9 cool **10** black **11** burnt **12** regular

Page 26 Direct speech (2)
A 1 "I am going home," said Mark.
2 "Bring my books, please," said Mr Mills.
3 "Are you hungry?" asked Mum.
4 "Stop that!" shouted the caretaker.
5 "Be very quiet," whispered Michael.
6 David asked, "Have you seen my cricket
bat?"
7 "Please close the door," he said. "Someone
may hear us."
8 Suddenly I stopped. "I've forgotten my
ticket," I said.

9 "Yes," shouted Bobby. "It's mine."

10 "It isn't fair," I cried. "You cheated."

11 Hazel said, "Aren't those roses beautiful?"

12 "Rosie said she couldn't stay," explained Leah.

B 1 "That doesn't belong to me," said Angus.

2 "Have you seen my dog?" Cathy asked.

3 "Try that coat on," suggested the shop assistant.

4 The old man looked very angry, "Get out!" he yelled.

5 "That's not hard!" he boasted, "Watch me do it."

6 "No Andrew," the coach said. "You are not shooting first time."

7 "Alex asked me to watch him," Stuart explained.

8 "Will you please carry this parcel for me?" asked the old lady.

9 "Where have you been? I've been waiting an hour for you," grumbled Rashid.

10 The answer Mr Davis gave me was, "You can't come in with your shoes on."

Page 27 Conjunctions

A 1 and **2** because **3** if **4** otherwise **5** until **6** whether **7** but **8** unless **9** when **10** so

B 1 because **2** since **3** although **4** wherever **5** since **6** while **7** when **8** until **9** and **10** but

Page 28 Vocabulary and spelling (2)

A 1 pain/pane **2** pale/pail **3** paws/pause **4** plaice/place

B 1 root/route **2** rows/rose **3** raise/rays **4** read/reed

C 1 son/sun **2** straight/strait **3** sow/sew **4** stile/style

Page 29 Mixed bag (3)

A The following words are possible answers. Check your child's answers and accept anything that has the same meaning as the word in bold.

1 avoided **2** accidentally **3** drought **4** improving **5** honest **6** reduced **7** inaudible **8** temporary **9** repeatedly **10** immediately

B 1 surgery **2** aviary **3** incubator **4** cinema **5** studio

C 1 musical instruments (plus your child's own addition)

2 meats (plus your child's own addition)

3 ball games/sports (plus your child's own addition)

4 boats (plus your child's own addition)

5 dogs (plus your child's own addition)

6 planets (plus your child's own addition)

7 colours (plus your child's own addition)

8 trees (plus your child's own addition)

9 clothes (plus your child's own addition)

10 furniture (plus your child's own addition)

Page 30 Occupations

A 1 chef **2** artist **3** optician **4** jockey **5** conductor **6** librarian **7** dentist **8** roofer/tiler/steeplejack **9** decorator

B 1 stationer **2** newsagent **3** florist **4** chemist **5** jeweller **6** butcher **7** fishmonger **8** baker

C 1 zookeeper **2** gardener **3** author **4** auctioneer **5** mechanic **6** hairdresser **7** sculptor **8** chiropodist

Page 31 Apostrophe – possession

A 1 Peter's pencil **2** the soldier's gun **3** the caretaker's brush **4** the farmer's field **5** Mr Clark's spade **6** the giraffe's neck **7** the designer's computer **8** the dog's dinner **9** the duck's feet **10** Sally's pen

B 1 the scouts' tents 2 the elephants' trunks 3 the flowers' petals 4 the sailors' submarine 5 the teachers' room 6 the footballers' boots 7 the astronauts' rocket 8 the birds' wings 9 the pilots' club 10 a dancers' school

C 1 the firefighters' helmets 2 the police officers' radios 3 the ladies' dresses 4 the babies' clothes 5 the neighbours' gardens 6 the thieves' hideout 7 the children's play area 8 the brothers' sister 9 the zoos' animals 10 the oxen's horns

D 1 the sheep's fleeces 2 the donkey's ears 3 the divers' masks 4 the bird's feathers 5 the women's club 6 the geese's wings

Page 32 Vocabulary and spelling (3)

A 1 precious 2 delicious 3 spacious 4 suspicious 5 unconscious

B 1 jewellery 2 millimetre 3 caterpillar 4 allotment 5 parallel

C 1 impossible 2 invisible 3 sensible 4 reversible 5 responsible

D 1 Christmas 2 chauffeur 3 chestnut 4 chrysalid 5 chiropodist

Page 33 Punctuation

A 1 Tom played squash with Terry on Monday night.
2 When Marie visited London she went in the Houses of Parliament.
3 Every Christmas Peter stays with his Aunty Edna in Nairobi.
4 Britain could import Jamaican sugar, New Zealand apples and Australian wool.
5 The busy holiday months in England are July and August.
6 Pelé, the famous footballer, played for Santos F.C. in Brazil and New York Cosmos.
7 Chloe's sister, Emma, is studying French at Sydney University.
8 In 2012 Queen Elizabeth II celebrated her Diamond Jubilee.

B 1 Morag, Sally and I went for a walk.
2 The cyclist, after a brief stop for food, resumed the race.
3 "If you see him, will you ask him to write?"
4 Some common metals are bronze, lead, iron and zinc.
5 Grandad, after a big dinner, went to sleep.
6 "Quick, march!" yelled the drill-sergeant.
7 "Are you feeling better today?" asked the teacher.
8 "What do you think you are doing?" shouted the angry farmer.

C 1 he will 2 she is 3 could not 4 will not 5 I am 6 you are 7 they have 8 who is

D 1 they're 2 you'd 3 she can't 4 that's 5 he shan't 6 where's 7 they'll 8 where've

Page 34 Mixed bag (4)

A 1 Please Turn Over 2 Police Constable 3 February 4 The Royal Society for the Prevention of Cruelty to Animals 5 leg before wicket 6 Avenue 7 before noon 8 Greenwich Mean Time 9 metres 10 kilometres per hour 11 for example 12 and other things 13 Very Important Person 14 European Union 15 centimetres

B 1 British 2 Canadian 3 Australian 4 Jamaican 5 Kenyan 6 Danish 7 Swiss 8 Finnish 9 Dutch

C 1 screech 2 squeak 3 bang 4 beat 5 rustle 6 clap

D 1 croak 2 hoot 3 bark 4 moo/low 5 neigh 6 bleat 7 chatter 8 purr/miaow

Page 35 Vocabulary – similar meanings

A **1** constantly **2** dilute **3** extinguish
4 exterior **5** pester **6** request **7** various
8 glorious **9** surrender **10** vivid **11** vacant
12 errors

B pull/haul, grind/crush, defend/guard, useless/futile, weak/feeble, encourage/support, polite/courteous, amaze/astound, buoyant/floating, compel/force, disappear/vanish, sincere/genuine

Page 36 Singular and plural

A **1** The boys have read their books.
2 We are going near Oban for our holidays.
3 The footballers wear red jerseys.
4 We shall sell them to the girls.
5 The girls tripped over the stones and hurt themselves.
6 The plays weren't very well acted.
7 We must help to feed the monkeys.
8 The men were very tired after they had worked hard in the gardens.
9 I saw geese in the fields.
10 These boys want to play chess.

B **1** My friend came on holiday with me.
2 The police officer checked his/her watch before he/she set off.
3 The knife had been sharpened.
4 A woman shouted at me.
5 The firefighter wears a uniform.
6 "Have you seen him/her?" I asked.
7 The chimpanzee is a very intelligent animal.
8 The first chapter of the book was missing.
9 I am sure you do not understand this idea.
10 I was pleased with the examination result which was published in the paper yesterday.

Page 37 Adverbs (3)

A **2** Joan answered quickly.
3 We sleep soundly.
4 Sam reads slowly.
5 The other team lost badly.
6 The sun shines brightly on the beach.
7 The explorer spoke interestingly.
8 Darren swims strongly.
9 The secretary answered promptly.
10 Rob played skilfully.

B **1** carefully **2** correctly **3** regularly
4 silently **5** promptly **6** generously
7 politely **8** finally **9** proudly **10** mentally

Page 38–39 Comprehension (1)

1 Brachen was overflowing because of the travellers and evacuees.
2 The green express connected Lucerne and Rome.
3 The time for the first news bulletin was seven.
4 Express trains weren't calling at Brachen because the Lucerne-Rome express train was stuck, waiting for the signal to change.
5 The railwaymen wore black overalls and black caps as uniforms.
6 The weather that particular morning was grey.
7 Two kinds of railway equipment kept round the station were cattle trucks and snow-ploughs.
8 The proprietor of the restaurant was a 'good' man because he handed his kitchen and coffee machine over to the Red Cross and let his employees work as volunteers.
9 The wireless was moved so that people could hear the latest news regarding threatened districts.
10 Paolo was half asleep because he was 'yawning his head off'.
11 This disaster took place in the mountains.
12a reports **b** thriving **c** reluctant **d** wireless **e** proprietor **f** volunteer **g** crammed **h** evacuees
13a The Red Cross was begun in 1864 by the Geneva Convention to provide medical care for war casualties and later to help victims of disasters, e.g. earthquakes.

b Pestalozzi Children's Villages were schools set up to care for refugee children after WW2. Pestalozzi was a Swiss educational reformer.

c Dewlaps are the loose bit of skin hanging from the neck of a dog or cattle.

Page 40 Adjectives (2)
A 1 thirsty **2** sleepy **3** stormy **4** showery
B 1 icy **2** shady **3** hazy **4** prickly
C 1 funny **2** muddy **3** furry **4** tinny
D 1 mischievous **2** skilful **3** expensive
4 dangerous
E 1 hasty **2** leaky **3** skinny **4** woolly
5 angry **6** poisonous **7** circular **8** juicy
9 accidental **10** dead **11** natural
12 expensive **13** sunny **14** sympathetic
15 deep

Page 41A One word for several
1 neighbours **2** bedroom **3** silently
4 queue **5** uncle **6** decided
7 autobiography **8** quarterly **9** famine
10 expand

B Incorrect sentences
1 Jamie played football with Peter and me.
2 Mr Peacock is the headmaster of a girls' school.
3 The cat was run over by a car.
4 Look at the baby drinking from its bottle.
5 Alan, Bob and Bill were sheltering from the storm.
6 I have earned fewer house marks this term.
7 "I didn't do anything wrong," sobbed Mark.
8 Our teacher said he would teach me to dive into the pool.
9 Frank is taller than the other two boys.
10 None of the pencils is sharp.

Page 42 Nouns and verbs – formation
A 1 announced **2** decided **3** admired
4 discovered **5** relieved **6** fed **7** discover
8 invite **9** grow **10** know

B 1 arrival **2** behaviour **3** entrance **4** injury
5 performance **6** delivery **7** explosion
8 obedience **9** invention **10** decision

Page 43 Mixed bag (5)
A Odd one out
1 listen **2** modern **3** school **4** early **5** hole
6 square **7** cautious **8** tutor **9** deadly
10 scatter **11** loosen **12** loiter

B Opposites
The following are possible answers. Accept anything that is opposite in meaning to those given.
1 brave **2** irregular **3** miniscule
4 considerate **5** rough **6** normal **7** vertical
8 careful **9** rare

C Rhyming words
1 weight **2** rein **3** stretch **4** howl **5** court
6 beat **7** healed **8** tent

Page 44 Vocabulary and spelling (4)
A 1 niece **2** handkerchief **3** ceiling **4** thief
5 believe **6** receive **7** piece **8** friend
9 deceive **10** height
B 1 dynamo **2** hyacinth **3** hyena
4 dynamite **5** python
C 1 equator **2** escalator **3** author
4 spectator **5** corridor

Page 45 Direct and indirect speech
A 1 Brian said he was tired after the long walk.
2 The caretaker said he'd lost his big brush.
3 The teacher said she'd/he'd lost her/his keys.
4 The teacher asked if anyone had found a bunch of keys.
5 Eric suggested that you could stay a little longer.
6 My dad advised me to try harder otherwise I'd never finish the job.
7 The old lady asked if you'd seen a black and white kitten.
8 Billy's friend warned him he mustn't play near the river.

9 He said he used to play for the first team.
10 Mr Thomas said he was sure that you hadn't listened.
B 1 The boys said, "We're sorry for being late."
2 Mum said, "Dinner is ready."
3 The pilot remarked, "It may be a bumpy flight."
4 Tom said, "I will not be able to play."
5 Dora asked, "Are you going to town?"
6 The secretary said, "The paper is mine."
7 The teacher said, "I won't be away long."
8 The farmer explained, "I'm going to dig some drains."
9 The boy asked, "Mr Aitken will you return my football?"
10 I asked Mr Perkins, "Where are you going in August?"

Page 46–47 Comprehension (2)

1 The different kinds of bats found by the writer are the Horseshoe, the Natterer's, the Whiskered, the Long-eared and the Barbastelle.
2 The most common bat was the Horseshoe.
3 The White-waistcoat and Whiskered Bats were the most difficult to capture because they wedged themselves deep in the crevices of the cave.
4 Bats feed on insects.
5 The Horseshoe Bats are deep sleepers.
6 The Barbastelle Bat makes a 'metallic buzz' sound.
7 The Natterer bat has a white underside whereas the Whiskered Bat is a dusky colour.
8 A chrysalid is a butterfly or moth at a stage between larva and adult, when it is surrounded by a cocoon. The cocoon is like the sleeping bat's wings.
9 The rarest bat found in the caves is the Barbastelle.
10a profoundly **b** species **c** still **d** noticeable **e** inhabits **f** dubbed **g** crying **h** afford **i** abundant **j** transparent

Page 48 Mixed bag (6)

A 1 lion **2** monkey **3** giraffe **4** zebra **5** camel **6** kangaroo
B 1 pea **2** potato **3** onion **4** carrot **5** turnip **6** cabbage
C 1 ash **2** oak **3** pine **4** beech **5** cedar **6** chestnut
D 1 incorrect **2** impossible **3** irregular **4** disobedient **5** unwrap **6** inconvenient **7** uncomfortable **8** impolite **9** unfortunate **10** inexperienced **11** discomfort **12** irresponsible
E 1 fastest **2** youngest **3** strongest **4** warmest **5** larger **6** better

Published by Collins
An imprint of HarperCollins*Publishers* Ltd
1 London Bridge Street
London
SE1 9GF

Browse the complete Collins catalogue at
www.collins.co.uk

First published in 1978
This edition first published in 2012

© Derek Newton and David Smith 2012

10 9 8 7 6 5

ISBN 978-0-00-750545-6

British Library Cataloguing in Publication Data.
A catalogue record for this publication is available from the British Library.

Project managed by Katie Galloway
Production by Rebecca Evans
Page layout by Exemplarr Worldwide Ltd
Illustrated by A. Rodger
Printed in Great Britain by Martins the Printers

MIX
Paper from responsible sources
FSC www.fsc.org
FSC C007454

FSC™ is a non-profit international organisation established to promote the responsible management of the world's forests. Products carrying the FSC label are independently certified to assure consumers that they come from forests that are managed to meet the social, economic and ecological needs of present and future generations, and other controlled sources.

Find out more about HarperCollins and the environment at
www.harpercollins.co.uk/green